THE PRACTICAL PROF:

SIMPLE LESSONS FOR ANYONE WHO WORKS

by

Santo D. Marabella, MBA, DSW

Dedication

To Mom & Dad,

Anna & Sam,

my first "profs"

Cover design: Nikki Ferlazzo
Illustrator: Joshua Graul
Author Photos: Steve G Photography

Acknowledgements

The narrative for the "Lessons" included in this book is used by permission of the *Reading Eagle*, where the original versions comprised the content for a monthly column in the *Business Weekly* published by the *Reading Eagle*. The author wishes to acknowledge Harry Deitz, Editor, for permission to use this material and to Daniel C. Fink, *Business Weekly* Editor, for his collaborative and mentoring editorial style in the preparation of the original articles.

✵✵✵

I am grateful to Moravian College for supporting this publication with a grant from the Amrhein Program & Faculty Enrichment Fund

✵✵✵

Nikki Ferlazzo and Joshua Graul, cover designer and illustrator, respectively, brought the fun but important messages to life with their incredible talents and wonderful artistic sensibilities.

✵✵✵

Brian M. Welsko, Research Assistant

✵✵✵

Thanks to Jake Cassaday, for friendship and support.

Catalogue Description

We are especially delighted that Dr. Santo D. Marabella has asked us to write this Foreword... ah, Catalog Description. We have known Dr. Marabella for over 30 years. He is part of our family.

In all of Santo's articles in this book, published originally in the *Reading Eagle*, he gets his points across in a pithy and poignant style. The tone is conversational, with an easy and enjoyable approach.

Anyone who has worked in a contemporary setting has probably found that today's environment is frequently populated with supervisors and co-workers whose styles, practices, and personalities do not allow for the most important element in the labor force: common sense. Employees find it difficult to put aside their own agendas for the benefit of the organization. Hence, the necessity for a Practical Professor!

The "lessons" in this book all relate, in one way or another, to common sense in the workplace with the intellectual know-how of Santo's extensive background and experience that makes this approach and philosophy a win/win with employment issues.

Santo writes about such topics as bullying in the workplace, workplaces to our homes, families and recreational spaces. Sometimes this carry-over takes the form of enthusiasm for work and love for one's accomplishments. Sometimes the carry-over is detrimental, taking the form of lingering emotional fatigue, stress, anxiety and overall dissatisfaction and unhappiness. The benefit of reading Santo's collection of lessons is in his practical approach for improving our working experiences.

But don't take our word for it. Read this book. Buy it for your supervisors. Give it to your adult kids (who hopefully are employed). Leave it in the break room, on your desk. Show it to your co-workers. Let them see you reading it on your break, and particularly laughing while you're doing so. Why? You and your co-workers can only gain from Santo's many years of expertise, and his practical approach to life experiences. These are the benefits of these lessons, which Santo now wants to share with all of us.

Carmela Capellupo-Beaver and Thomas W. Beaver, Esq.

A Message from the "Prof"

Thank you for your interest in *The Practical Prof: Simple Lessons for Anyone Who Works*. I hope that it will be an enjoyable and educational experience!

I do want you to think of me as your personal work-life advisor. Whether it is in challenging economic times or times of growth, having a "prof" that stays with you while you work can be a great perk. I really believe the best teaching and learning are also fun. I think this approach has the best chance of causing enduring life-long learning and growth. I have always been a believer in edutainment – education that is also entertaining. I hope that you have found this book to be both.

I look forward to hearing from you, seeing and talking with you online during my Office Hours, and perhaps connecting with you and your company at a future speaking engagement. Feel free to be in touch and thanks for studying with *The Practical Prof*.

Santo D. Marabella, MBA, DSW
The Practical Prof
santo@ThePracticalProf.com
www.ThePracticalProf.com

Syllabus

Keeping the Lessons Alive

As *The Practical Prof*, Dr. Santo D. Marabella believes his simple lessons, told in an entertaining way, can have a meaningful impact on how you work, or you manage your employees and their workplace. Marabella also believes that interactive, participative learning is the best approach for keeping the lessons alive and applicable to your daily work-life. With that in mind, this book aims to be a practical read and the centerpiece for an interactive dialogue. To facilitate this interaction and participation, *The Practical Prof* suggests a number of simple steps.

First, embrace the **Lesson Mantras** that follow each lesson. Let them guide and inspire you so that you stay present to the lesson's ideas and concepts.

Second, scribble your comments and reflections in the **Personal Notes** section of each lesson. Don't worry about how they look or if they are properly worded – this is just for you to reinforce what you think and what you have learned.

Next, refer to the **Resources** listed at the end of each lesson when you want to learn more. They will lead you to details about information presented in the lessons, or expand on the topics discussed. On the Home Page at www.ThePracticalProf.com, just click on the Book Resources link. When prompted, enter this password: **Re$ourcesTPP**, and you will find a roster of articles, publications, websites, and other resources referenced in the book (when available, hyperlinks are provided). The list will be updated when new resources that are credible and relevant are identified. Readers are invite to submit resources they have as well.

Fourth, consider the questions and comments in the **Questions to Consider** section of each Lesson. The objective is not to have you agree with everything in the Lesson, but to be open to thinking differently and challenging your "mental models" or previously held perceptions.

Then, do the **Homework** offered at the end of each Lesson. This is where you put the content of each Lesson to work *at work*. Simple, incremental or subtle changes can have significant, positive payoffs. And, sometimes, just being present (conscious) to an issue can make a big difference.

Sixth, enroll in The Practical Prof's **Office Hours** – a monthly, live streaming video conference for all readers where you can video chat with the author and other readers about the book, the topic of the day and your own questions. You can enroll on the website. Schedule and enrollment details are available by clicking on the Office Hours link on the Home Page at www.ThePracticalProf.com. All you will need is this book's ISBN# found on the back cover. Remember, all readers receive a *free two-month trial* to Office Hours.

Finally, check out the regular monthly column, The Practical Prof, featured the third Tuesday of every month in the Business Weekly of the Reading Eagle newspaper:

http://businessweekly.readingeagle.com/?s=santo+marabella

Introducing Lavo!

It is a pleasure to introduce you to Lavo, (short for "lavoro" - Italian for "work"). Lavo will guide you through the Lessons in this book. He has a lot of knowledge and experience with these Lessons, so enjoy his visual "commentary" throughout your study with The Practical Prof.

LESSON #1: Put a "P" for Passion in your work!

LESSON #1: Put a "P" for Passion in your work!

"Work" has always been a four-letter word. Unfortunately for many employees since the advent of the "merger mania" of the '90s, this word has taken on the pejorative properties of the most profane four-letter words. There are many contributing factors, but I'll focus on just one.

Passion.

Passion is the "P" that should be in work but is so often nowhere to be found, and at great cost. According to a recent Forbes article, failing to find a project for the talent that ignites an employee's passion is the No. 2 reason among the top 10 for why large companies fail to keep their best talent. But when the spark of passion is present, it can be directly correlated to peak performance, low turnover and long-term commitment to the organization.

So, what is passion, and how do you inspire your team to have it? Passion is what makes work meaningful. It motivates people to get up at 3 a.m. It gives people energy when their tank is on "E." It engenders pride and satisfaction, builds self-confidence and contributes to competence.

It's also unique to each individual. And that can make it challenging to identify in every employee. But it's part of your job as a manager or business owner to help each employee discover his passion and create opportunities to be fulfilled through it. That means giving employees the time and space to experiment, and even to play; -- to approach their work with a Zen Buddhist's "beginner's mind" and all the wonder and exploration that accompanies it.

I'm not suggesting a no-holds-barred free-for-all; just a deliberate and consistent effort to infuse your employees' passion into your work environment.

Here's how I discovered my own professional passion. When I was a grad student, I taught a course just to make some money to pay for school. I thought it was just a means to an end, until I was actually in the classroom. During and after that first course, I thought about the experience of teaching and what it really meant to me. I got excited about the material I was teaching and equally excited that I was able to get students engaged in the learning as well. I didn't mind the long drive home, the late night classes or the complaints of some students. I was energized being in the classroom and saw meaning in the end product of my efforts: I had an impact on students. I realized rather quickly that the monetary compensation for that course, and for this career, was not a driving force. I knew, with my credentials, I could earn a lot more money in business than I ever could as an educator. But, because teaching is my passion, it didn't matter. Or at least the money didn't matter enough to ignore my passion and go try to have a career doing something else.

Have a conversation with your people about what "lights them up" in their professional world. Encourage them to talk with each other, eliminate failure from your business-speak, enable them to do what is necessary in ways that engage more of them in the task and let them do things that may not be necessary, if they can make a good business case for the actions they propose. And, before you discount this as business hooey, think about your own career. What if you didn't have passion for your work? How invested would you be? Oh, if that question hits a slightly dissonant chord with you personally, then you may want to join your team on this journey.

If you find ways to add a "P" to the way you and your team spells w-o-r-k, I believe your workplace will nurture and sustain a more productive and engaged staff of high performers, and many intended and surprising benefits become possible.

LESSON MANTRA

If I help co-workers connect with my passion, they will share and support my vision.

PERSONAL NOTES:

QUESTIONS TO CONSIDER

It's been said that "a master in the art of living draws no sharp distinctions between his work and his play" (Chateaubriand or LP Sacks, both are credited), or put another way, "the supreme accomplishment is to blur the line between work and play (Arnold J. Toynbee). Does this describe your work-life? If not, what would it take to discover your passion or integrate it in your work-life so that you play at work?

If you say that it is not feasible to have passion in your work, where else can you or do you live passionately?

HOMEWORK

Identify your passion. If you aren't sure what your passion is, answer the following question:

- For what one thing would I get up early, stay up late, forget to eat over, postpone being with my favorite people – all with no (or minimal) complaints about?

The answer is your passion. You say there's more than one? Always great to have choices!

Now that you have your passion, pick 2 people in your life – one from work, one from non-work ☺ - who you trust and share your passion with them (tell them it's an assignment from your "prof," they'll understand).

Next, celebrate your passion. It doesn't have to be public or a big deal. It can be as simple as writing it down, giving yourself an award (yes, that's what I said), or designating a "passion day" (ok, hour) for yourself. For example, my passion is teaching. To celebrate my passion, I might write on a piece of paper "I LOVE TEACHING" and put it on my bulletin board in my office. If I'm feeling really creative, I might make a certificate that says, "Best Teacher in the Universe" with my name boldly printed; or, if I'm really in a celebratory mood, I might read an article, go to a conference, talk with a colleague about how to grow and develop as a teacher.

Sound silly? Try it, and then tell me how silly it was. You'll be amazed at the self-affirming energy and power you'll create.

RESOURCES

Denning, S. (2007). *The secret language of leadership.* San Francisco, CA: John Wiley & Sons.

Jackson, E. (14 Dec 2011). Top ten reasons why large companies fail to keep their best talent. *Forbes.* http://www.forbes.com/sites/ericjackson/2011/12/14/top-ten-reasons-why-large-companies-fail-to-keep-their-best-talent/

Robinson, K. (2009). *The element.* London, England: Penguin.

Weinstein, M. (1997). *Managing to have fun. .* New York, NY: Fireside.

LESSON #2: The elusive transition from entrepreneur to manager

LESSON #2: The elusive transition from entrepreneur to manager

So you always wanted to be your own boss and had this great idea for a business. You are creative, resourceful, self-motivated and assertive. And you can enroll people in your vision and transform ideas into marketable products or services. Sounds like you're an entrepreneur.

Fast-forward about three years.

Your sales are flat or down, product or service quality is inconsistent and innovation is nonexistent. Yeah, your business is surviving, but you're bored. After some reflection, you realize you don't like to plan, you're not that well organized, you're uncomfortable supervising others and the elements of business control, such as budgets and quality, for example, really cramp your style. Sounds like you're not a manager.

Unfortunately, as many entrepreneurs have found out the hard way, the skill set that launches innovative small businesses is not necessarily enough to keep it going successfully. That skill set is about management.

So what's the difference between entrepreneurship and management?

Entrepreneurship comprises several stages. It's a classification of activities that must be undertaken in sequence. Put another way, the stages of entrepreneurship are achieved in ways similar to building a house or changing a flat tire. You have to do step one before step two, and so on.

The stages of entrepreneurship range from three to six, depending on the author you consult: David Bozward, Jon Gillespie-Brown and Jim Collins, the "Good to Great" guru, are three. Their basic themes are all essentially the same: Develop an idea, create a plan to transform the idea into a business, start the business and grow the business. You can see how these skills are applicable to the stages, at least the first three stages.

But, we need to look a bit closer at the fourth stage, growing your business. Most authors agree that it usually takes about three years to reach an adequate level of growth. And while the experts agree that growth is key to sustaining a successful business, they don't exactly agree about how that is done.

In my opinion, that's because this is where entrepreneurship ends and management begins.

Again, as with the entrepreneurship experts, authors of management books such as Stephen P. Robbins, Mary Coulter and Gary Hamel have many ways of describing this process. Generally, the management process is most frequently categorized into four functions: planning, organizing, leading and control. Briefly defined, planning encompasses the activities of creating purpose, setting goals and making decisions; organizing involves determining the structure and design and managing change; leading means understanding individual and group behavior in order to motivate and communicate with employees; and planning and implementing methods of financials, information and quality equal control.

Where the stages of entrepreneurship are sequential, once a business is under way, one or more of the functions of management can be called into play at any given time. You could argue that these functions also have a sequence to them. You have to create your purpose, or plan, before you can determine your organization structure, or organize, and so on. That is true — at the beginning of an organization's life. But once an organization is established, management functions operate constantly.

In the tension between the entrepreneur and the manager, there's a little bit of yin and yang.

Entrepreneurs create, innovate and build; managers systematize, monitor and evaluate. Entrepreneurs accept risk and change as the status quo; managers minimize risk and manage change to sustain the status quo. Entrepreneurs attract resources; managers allocate or deploy resources. Simply put, entrepreneurs get things started; managers keep things going.

As an example, I was the founding Executive Director for Leadership Berks, a community leadership development program for individuals from area businesses who are committed to making a difference. The Steering Committee that founded LB developed a training program for Berks County's community leaders (create/innovate); targeted businesses to send their employees and pay for them to go (accept risk); and brought funding, volunteers and staff to the program (attract resources). Much of the focus and energy of my 12-year tenure was spent working with the board to establish policies and procedures (systemize), make purchases within the bounds of a budget (allocate resources) and, review and improve the program content (monitor and evaluate). Committee members were the entrepreneurs, I was the manager.

To me, the best organizations and companies are led by entrepreneurs and managers. If you can't or don't want to do both, make sure you partner with someone who can complement your role and ensure that entrepreneurship and management permeate every fiber of your organization's being. This will give you the best chance of keeping your entrepreneurial spirit alive, as well as your company.

LESSON MANTRA

As an entrepreneur, I have the autonomy to create and the responsibility to manage – I need to excel at both!

PERSONAL NOTES:

QUESTIONS TO CONSIDER

Are you a manager or an entrepreneur? Both? Neither?

If you are both, in which role are you more comfortable? Why?

If neither, which role would you like to take on sometime in the future? Why?

HOMEWORK

If you are an entrepreneur who has and runs their own business and has employees, ask them to answer the following questions:

- What can I (you, their boss, not me, your "prof") do to become a better manager?
- How can I help you do your job better (as in, easier, faster, and more effectively)?
- What's great about working at our company?
- What do you wish would be different about working here?

Yeah, I get that this might be a difficult and awkward task (especially if you have only one or two employees and worry about anonymity). But, wouldn't it be better to know what your employees think, instead of being oblivious to issues that if addressed, could help your business?

And, if you don't have employees, ask your customers these questions (same as above, just tweaked for the different audience):

- What can I do to become a better vendor, supplier, producer, provider (fill in the appropriate term)?
- How can I help you be more successful in your business (your customer's business)?

- What is great about doing business with our company?
- What do you wish would be different about doing business with us?

My hunch is that any areas for improvement or development, identified by your employees or customers, will be management issues, not entrepreneurial issues. The issues will likely be about planning, leading, organizing and control – the four functions I described in this lesson.

If you're not an entrepreneur, and have always thought about starting your own business, I have some questions for you:

- What business would you start? Why?
- Is it built upon a passion of yours?
- What is stopping you from starting this business? (Oh, and "not enough money" is not an acceptable response – I get that it's an issue, it's just not a reason not to do something because we never have the money to do what we want, but we still do many things that we want, and the money comes)
- What one step can you take in the next three days to explore starting your own business?

Not interested in being an entrepreneur or a manager? No worries – better to know yourself that well, than to force yourself to do or be something that will not give you satisfaction.

RESOURCES

Bozward, D. (2011). *The motivated entrepreneur.* Great Britain: Zenga.

Collins, J. C., & Lazier, W. C. (1992). *Beyond entrepreneurship.* Paramus, NJ:
    Prentice Hall.

Gillespie-Brown, J. (2009). *So you want to be an entrepreneur?* Chichester, UK:
    Capstone.

Hamel, G. (2007). *The future of management.* Boston, MA: Harvard Business
    School Publishing.

Robbins, S. P., & Coulter, M. (2012). *Management.* Upper Saddle River: NJ:
    Prentice Hall.

LESSON #3: Bullying in the workplace

LESSON #3: Bullying in the workplace

Think bullying stops after high school? Think again. Bullying isn't just a school problem, it's a social problem found everywhere, including the workplace. In fact, the Workplace Bullying Institute reports that in 2010 about 35 percent of employees in the U.S. had been or are currently being bullied. That's more than one-third of employees.

Let's take a closer look at workplace bullying and what can be done to minimize and eventually eliminate bullying at work.

To really understand the issue, we need to be open to seeing bullying differently than we previously may have thought. A team of colleagues and I presented a symposium on bullying to 200 social-work practitioners and agency leaders at University of Penn's School of Social Policy and Practice in 2012. We had nine presenters, including practitioners and researchers, but also bullies and victims of bullying. Here is what we learned.

First, bullying is a pattern of harassment or incivility that is as disempowering to the bully as it is to the victim. Second, the more attention and resources we invest in the bully, the better our chance for eliminating this behavior. Third, bullying is a social problem, not a rite of passage, which occurs across the lifespan and victimizes kids, adults and the elderly. Fourth, bullying stops when people start speaking up.

What does bullying look like in the workplace? It may surprise you that most workplace bullies are bosses, and most victims are workplace "stars," the most popular or respected employees. Consider that these types of employees pose the greatest threat to the incompetent or insecure bullying boss. And, part of the reason workplace bullying may be so pervasive is that employees' fears of losing their job in this market is stronger than the anxiety and stress caused by being bullied.

In case you're worried that I'm giving carte blanche to employees who want to misrepresent their strict or stern boss as a bully, I offer this distinction. Srini Pillay, assistant clinical professor of psychiatry at Harvard Medical School and author of "Life Unlocked: 7 Revolutionary Lessons To Overcome Fear," states that the difference between a stern person and a bullying boss lies in their intentions. The strict boss acts for the good of the company and/or the employee, while the bullying boss is most concerned with his own welfare and interests. Pillay elaborates on the differences by pointing out that a bullying boss is aggressive, overcompensates for his own lack of esteem and is prone to humiliate.

Workplace bullying can manifest itself in many forms. It can involve verbal (ridiculing or maligning a person), physical (pushing, shoving or threatening physical assault), gestural (nonverbal glances to scare) and exclusionary tactics (not inviting a person to a relevant business meeting).

What can we do? I offer a number of recommendations.

I am reminded of a consulting project I did for Lucent Technologies in 2000 related to workplace violence, a possible outcome of workplace bullying. Even though the firm is no longer in business, client confidentiality precludes me from revealing any specific data about the project. But, I can say that Lucent impressed me for this reason. It was proactive in dealing with workplace violence. It engaged me to explore the issue with employees, not as a reaction to any particular incident, but as a strategy for preventing violence from occurring and for managing any incidents, if they did occur.

This is my first recommendation. Be proactive. Have a plan before you have a problem.

Next, establish a written policy of zero tolerance. In the policy, state that bullying is forbidden, describe bullying behaviors relevant to your workplace and be clear that this policy applies to all employees. Then post it on your website and share it, using the media your company uses to communicate important information.

Third, be sure you have an organizational culture that supports and encourages enforcement. In other words, if you expect employees to report bullying — theirs or incidents they observe — you can't dismiss, diminish or, worst of all, penalize them for doing so. Create a safe way for employees to report bullying they have experienced or witnessed.

Fourth, if bullying does occur, pay attention to and address the needs of the bully as well as the victim. Am I suggesting that we get the bully therapy or counseling? Maybe. In most cases, it may not be appropriate for an employer to require an employee to get help. But, in my opinion, facilitating opportunities for personal growth and development, including anger management classes, counseling, workshops, etc., is well within the purview of a company's responsibilities to its employees.

Some readers may be concerned that I have too much empathy for the bully. As one who was bullied in school, it is personally challenging to endorse a strategy of care and support for the bully. However, I know that people who are free from their demons and insecurities do not bully. By "free," I don't mean without impact, just that they are not dominated or controlled by them. If we can help the bully become stronger than his demons, we have a good chance of helping him not bully.

Fifth, if you are victimized or witness bullying, by all means speak up. I understand that someone who is a victim of bullying may feel embarrassed or stigmatized by having to admit and report this. And I know there are many disincentives, such as being ostracized or demeaned — also a form of bullying — for speaking up about bullying you witness or know exists.

The power of changing behavior begins, or never occurs, because of one person's choice to take a stand.

Finally, get outside help from reputable sources if you need it. There are many good sources of information and resources available for understanding and stopping workplace bullying. The ones I most recommend are the Workplace Bullying Institute (www.workplacebullying.org) and the Center for Workforce Studies of the National Association of Social Workers (workforce.socialworkers.org).

Managers and employees have a clear choice: Stand by, observe and pity, or step in, speak up and stop. The first choice perpetuates oppression in the workplace. It defends bullying. The second choice empowers and promotes dignity and respect in the workplace. It defends individual freedom. There are no convenient loopholes or gray areas to hide behind in this business scenario.

So, whose side are you on?

LESSON MANTRA

I am the trustee of the power my position and personality give me and use my power to protect, elevate, restore and develop individual dignity in my workplace.

PERSONAL NOTES:

QUESTIONS TO CONSIDER

Have you ever been bullied by your boss or co-worker? Have you ever
bullied anyone at work?

Have you made peace and got closure – at least with yourself, if not also with your bully or your victim? Closure and peace can be achieved as simply as not blaming yourself (if you were bullied), or forgiving yourself (if you were the bully).

Do you speak up or take action to protect co-workers who have been bullied? If not, what could you do to make it "safe" for you to stop bullying in your workplace? ("Nothing" is not an acceptable answer. There is always something that you can do.)

HOMEWORK

Find out if your workplace has a policy for zero tolerance of bullying. If you're the boss, that should be easy to do, if not, start with your Human Resources or Personnel department (for smaller companies and NFPs, ask the owner, CEO or executive director.

If there is a policy, ask if the policy could be the topic of a future staff meeting, workshop or professional development session. If there is no policy, write one. Obviously, you will need to follow the appropriate protocol for establishing workplace policies, which is different in every organization. But, do it. Even if it never gets approved, you will have made the issue discussable and brought it to the organization's "consciousness" and perhaps, conscience.

RESOURCES

Einarsen, S., Raknes, B. I., & Matthiesen, S. B. (1994). Bullying and harassment at work and their relationships to work environment quality: an exploratory study. *European work and organizational psychologist*, 4(4), 381-401. DOI: 10.1080/13594329408410497

Pillay, S. (2010). *Life Unlocked: 7 revolutionary lessons to overcome fear.* New York, NY: Rodale.

Results of the 2010 and 2007 WBI U.S. workplace bullying survey. *Workplace Bullying Institute*. http://www.workplacebullying.org/wbiresearch/2010-wbi-national-survey/

Whitaker, T. (2012). Social workers and workplace bullying: perceptions, responses and implications. *Work,* 42(1), 115-23.

LESSON #4: Tough problem at work? Deal with it!

LESSON #4: Tough problem at work? Deal with it!

Imagine the worst corporate nightmare: a tampered or defective product or a financial scandal. OK, and then consider the impact on your employees, customers, reputation and sales. Makes you squirm a bit, huh?

Now, imagine the adverse impact multiplied exponentially. Reaching for the Tums™ yet? Good. You're right where I want you to be: where you wind up when you avoid or ignore serious problems in your organization.

Not exactly Disneyland, is it?

Obviously, I'm talking about the worst kind of problems a company might be faced with: theft, embezzlement, bullying, harassment of any type, ignoring real safety concerns. Criminal or immoral activity.

Here are a few notorious examples:

Ford knew about the design problem with its Pinto in 1978, but did nothing until wrongful-death lawsuits forced the recall and eventual elimination of the model in 1981.

The landmark tobacco industry settlement of 1998 cost tobacco companies more than $246 billion in their agreements with the states because they refused to acknowledge their products' devastating health impact.

Deceptive accounting practices and fraud led to Lehman Brothers' 2008 bankruptcy.

In all of these cases, there were people in the organization who knew what was going on, but they refused to deal with it.

To be fair, there are some other high-profile cases involving Enron, WorldCom and the FBI in which people did take action. As a result, the problems were addressed, but at great personal costs: their jobs, reputations and mental health.

And remember the tampered Tylenol crisis of 1982? Even if you don't, I bet you've heard of Tylenol. That's because Johnson & Johnson, the makers of the analgesic, took swift and comprehensive action: It recalled every Tylenol product, reformulated the actual tablet and redesigned the packaging. The Tylenol brand, unlike the Pinto, survived because the company dealt with the problem.

So if companies are faced with obviously serious problems, why are they being ignored? We could make a list of reasons, but I'm only going to focus on one: fear.

Let's look at Penn State University and the Roman Catholic Church. In my opinion, Penn State and the Catholic Church shared the same systemic, organization-wide (at least in terms of where organizational power lies) fear: the fear that to deal with it would jeopardize the integrity, reputation and future of an entire institution.

But look at what not dealing with it has done. Both are examples of what occasionally happens in American business. Employees, even those at the top, are often afraid to stand up or speak up because of the potential negative consequences: damage to corporate and personal reputations or lost revenue. In some cases, it takes criminal investigations or lawsuits to spur action.

Both institutions will survive. Hopefully, both have learned at least two important lessons. One, in any institution, it is everyone's responsibility to ensure that everyone is safe and protected. Two, confronting the problem openly produces an outcome that is far better than avoiding the problem (bad) or covering it up (worse).

Your company may be a small business or corporation, but there are still great costs of not dealing with problems. A 2010 study by corporate trainers VitalSmarts found that 95 percent of employees struggle to speak up about concerns. And not surprisingly, the study confirmed that the few employees who do discuss crucial issues waste significantly less time complaining, feeling sorry for themselves, avoiding problems and getting angry.

So why do those 95 percent have a hard time voicing their concerns? We don't have to look further than our boss or our organization's culture to get our answer. Ask yourself, at your company: How safe is it to express different opinions? What happens to individuals who speak up? How much pressure is there to, as Landmark Education would put it, "look good" and "avoid looking bad" at all costs?

Reflecting on these questions may unlock the key for your organization to deal with it in a good way. Doing nothing, well, I think you know where that takes you.

And it's not Disneyland.

LESSON MANTRA

Inaction, avoidance and ignorance are not options when faced with difficult problems. I will be proactive and responsive in anticipating and addressing workplace problems.

PERSONAL NOTES:

QUESTIONS TO CONSIDER

Whether you are a manager or not, do you tend to avoid dealing with problems at work? (Be honest, no one will know how you answer!)

If you are an avoider, do you know why? Does your answer include – I don't want to hurt anyone's feelings, I hate confrontations, I don't think I should have to deal with people problems on top of everything else? If so, you're not alone.

Now, think of a situation where you experienced the impact of someone who did not take action to solve a workplace problem. How did that go for you? Remember what you expected from your manager or the person with authority to take action. It probably wasn't un-reasonable – more like, just want to be treated fairly or respected or supported. Use that memory to motivate your future actions.

HOMEWORK

If you've already read some of the Homework from other Lessons, you might think that in this assignment, I'm going to ask you to go create a problem and deal with it. Well, you're right... kinda.

What I'd actually like you to do is run an inventory of past or ongoing problems through your mind, and pick one that isn't solved or hasn't been addressed. It could be a comment you made or someone said to you that you think caused hurt feelings; it could be feedback on your last performance review that you didn't understand or agree with; or, it could be a co-worker who does something slightly annoying like stands in your cube while you're on a phone call waiting to ask you a question.

Got a situation? Now take some action. Go talk to the person – ask them for clarification, take responsibility for insensitive comments, let them know your feelings were hurt. You might be concerned that showing such vulnerability will be perceived as a weakness, and it might be, to a person who is insecure. But, actually, being expressed and "cleaning up" lingering problems will more likely be empowering to you, and maybe even to the other person.

RESOURCES

Daynard, R. A., Parment, W., Kelder, G., & Davidson, P. (2001). Implications for tobacco control of the multistate tobacco settlement. *American Journal of Public Health.* 91(12), 1967-71.

Lacayo, R. & Ripley, A. (30 December 2002). Persons of the year 2002: the whistleblowers. *Time Magazine.* http://www.time.com/time/magazine/article/0,9171,1003998,00.html

Lee, M. T. (1998). The ford pinto case and the development of auto safety regulations, 1893-1978. *Business and Economic History.* (27)2, 390-401.

Rehak, J. (23 March 2002). Tylenol made a hero of Johnson & Johnson: the recall that started them all. *The New York Times.* http://www.nytimes.com/2002/03/23/your-money/23iht-mjj_ed3_.html

Silent danger: the five crucial conversations that drive safety. (2009). *VitalSmarts.* http://cms.vitalsmarts.com/d/d/workspace/SpacesStore/27d878da-a919-46c2-9f44-f9516926b91b/Silent%20Danger%20-%20Safety%20Study%20Executive%20Summary.pdf?guest=true

Sorkin, A. R. (14 September 2008). Lehman files for bankruptcy; Merrill is sold. *The New York Times.* http://www.nytimes.com/2008/09/15/business/15lehman.html?pagewanted=all&_r=0

LESSON #5: Stop and think before you "Send."

LESSON #5: Stop and think before you "Send."

"Well, at least we don't have to worry, now that we know Santo is not going to chair the committee."

This is an excerpt from an email sent by a colleague, whom I'll call Careless Colleague, sent to another colleague but inadvertently copied to the entire faculty. Apparently Careless Colleague wasn't comfortable with my leadership style and couldn't help but celebrate that I chose not to accept the role. As you can imagine, I was embarrassed, though not nearly as embarrassed as Careless was!

Those emails you wish you could pull back, they happen. I asked readers for some feedback on careless and impulsive emails sent or received. Here are a few examples you provided:

A co-worker made a date over email with her boyfriend with details of how they would have a "good time" and sent it to all employees, not just the boyfriend. While it was not graphic, she was so embarrassed that she left work early that day.

"I disagreed on ethical grounds with a colleague's decision about how to charge a customer. That colleague sent an email to me, copying our respective bosses, complaining that I should not have given my opinion on this issue. I responded with an angry email to my colleague but did not copy our bosses. She replied, with copies to our bosses, in what became an ugly email chain. Our working relationship has suffered ever since."

"I am a consultant and sent a request to a client for some help in acquiring a contact list. The client responded, 'Isn't that what we're paying you to do?' I responded, 'Sure, no problem, I'll be glad to find the info,' which was followed by the client's reply, 'No, I was only kidding!' It is really difficult to read tone into email."

In reviewing all of the examples, two words come to mind: careless and impulsive. We really need to get a hold of ourselves around the matter of one tiny button: "send." I mean, really, is it that hard to control ourselves? Apparently so.

Email is such a quick and efficient way to communicate that it is easy to get careless about reviewing or thinking about what we are sending. And it is so tempting to get caught up in the short-lived but exhilarating feeling of vengeance: You embarrassed me, so I'm going to embarrass you more; you attacked me, so I'm fighting back; and, finally, I just want to engage in good old-fashioned gossip.

I'm not sure that Careless Colleague really cared about the impact of the message on me or on Careless' own reputation, but I think most of us do. So, consider these two observations and some suggestions about how to be responsible in controlling our inner send button.

First, I notice that many of these types of emails are reactions, not responses. We get an email message that annoys, angers, embarrasses — fill in your verb — and we react, in much the same way that people escalate arguments to shouting matches. The difference with email is the advantage of distance. We're not in the same physical space, or at least not face to face, which means we don't have to reply immediately. Just because we can have nearly real-time conversations by email and instant messenger doesn't mean we should.

Second, email is often knowingly and inappropriately used in place of in-person, face-to-face communication. Why? At work, we are often cowards. We seem to lack the integrity and courage to communicate directly with co-workers when negative or bad news or issues need to be discussed. Remember that disagreement I mentioned above about a colleague and myself? Instead of shooting off an angry note, I should have just walked over and talked to her.

What can we do to control our inner send button? Here are a few recommendations:

1. Stop, pause, and just don't send it. In other words, take a breath. Oxygen helps us think more clearly, and the pause gives us the space to be more thoughtful and deliberate.

2. Get some distance from the email/tweet/post. Yes, real distance, as in "turn off your email, go for a walk, hang out at the water cooler and discuss last night's game" distance.

3. Ask a person you trust to read it for tone, content and possible negative consequences. The key here is a person you trust, meaning someone who will look out for you and advise you objectively.

4. Rewrite or at least re-read. After you have worked through suggestions 1, 2 and 3, you are ready for No. 4. Re-reading and rewriting now can actually be done effectively.

5. Don't send it. If you have any gut feeling of concern, seriously reconsider if the message should be sent at all. When is your gut wrong? Listen to it over your ego every time.

6. Try face-to-face. If you feel the content of what you were trying to say should still be communicated, explore other modes of communication, perhaps even — hold onto your seat — in person. When you actually talk to someone directly, you'll be amazed at the power given and shared in such a conversation.

Consider the suggestions above as a strategy for replacing "careless" and "impulsive" with "thoughtful" and "deliberate." I know you don't want to be a Careless Colleague.

LESSON MANTRA

I will be a Carefully Communicative Colleague – thoughtful, deliberate and reasonable in all of my workplace communications.

PERSONAL NOTES:

QUESTIONS TO CONSIDER

Have you ever sent or received an email that should have been "stopped" before it was "sent?" If you were the sender, how long did the feeling of vindication or revenge last? If you were the receiver, how long did the disempowering feelings last?

HOMEWORK

One way to prevent careless or impulsive communications is to have what I call a "trusted screener." A trusted screener is someone you trust (yes, I know that part is obvious) to review any communications – written or verbal *before* (not during or after) the communication is sent. They will honestly tell you if you should proceed with the communication, modify it, or delete the entire message and take a walk. And, you will follow their counsel – no if's, and's or but's.

Designate who will be your trusted screener – the person at work (or at home, but who reviews touchy work communications) who will review any written or verbal communication you want to send. Make sure they know that you expect them to tell you what you need to hear, not necessarily what you want to hear. In this assignment, I'm not going to ask you to create a situation to practice this, just have the conversation with your trusted screener so that you're ready when the next situation arises – and don't worry, one will arise!

RESOURCES

Husted, B. (13 April 2013). Think before you email. *The Atlanta Journal-Constitution.* http://www.ajc.com/news/lifestyles/think-before-you-email/nXHsz/

Savitz, E. (6 June 2012). Think before you send: the legal risks in casual e-mail. *Forbes.* http://www.forbes.com/sites/ciocentral/2012/06/06/think-before-you-send-the-legal-risks-in-casual-e-mail/

Tugend, A. (20 April 2012). What to think about before you hit 'send'? *The New York Times. http://www.nytimes.com/2012/04/21/your-money/what-to-think-about-before-you-hit-send.html?pagewanted=all*

US News & World Report Tribune Media Services. (8 April 2011). Face time may beat e-mail. *Chicago Tribune.* http://www.chicagotribune.com/features/tribu/ct-tribu-call-dont-email,0,3906142.story

LESSON #6: Customer service solution - make it an act.

LESSON #6: Customer service solution - make it an act.

There's a crime of epic proportions being committed in our country. It affects our children, our communities, our jobs and most of all it threatens everything we believe in — revealing a new level of atrocity in man's inhumanity to man…and woman.

The crime: crappy customer service.

The victim: everyone who seeks support, assistance, guidance, clarification and just a friendly ear or a warm smile or a thoughtful remark from companies, businesses and stores in the U.S.

Think I'm exaggerating? Take a look at some of these submitted by our readers.

A pregnant customer, with a 3 year old in tow, shops for vacuum cleaners, which are displayed on an inaccessible shelf. A worker called to help gets a call on his phone about refrigerators and abandons her, without a word. Big help!

The regulatory compliance department of a mortgage-service firm was having difficulty keeping up with the Do Not Call database, and accidentally and repeatedly called a mortgage customer to cross-sell products. That customer happened to be an attorney who threatened the company with a class-action lawsuit. The mortgage company improved its data management, but not before paying off the customer's mortgage.

A woman had a death in her family and needed to fly home quickly. She had a free ticket on a no-frills airline. She was told there were no free seats available on the flight; however, she could purchase a seat for $900 on that flight. She questioned why if there was a seat available, she couldn't use her free ticket in this emergency. Their response: "We don't have any bereavement policies because we are a low-cost airline." Her wallet $900 lighter, she was back East grieving more than her family loss.

Ever want to rewrite the "script" on scenes such as these?

The good news is: Good service does sometimes happen. The call center rep really gets your frustration in receiving the wrong online order for the second time because the rep understands being disappointed.

The wait staff notices you didn't finish much of your meal and asks if everything is okay.

The store clerk believes you when you explain that the flat screen TV was cracked when you took it out of the box and that you didn't drop it.

The auto mechanic just won't give up trying to find where that "squealing" noise is coming from under your hood because he is committed to solving problems.

The auto mechanic just won't give up trying to find where that "squealing" noise is coming from under your hood because he is committed to solving problems.

So it is possible to rewrite that bad script. You can do it by adapting theater for customer-service training. As a community theater director and playwright, I believe every customer-service job has a character, much like a character in a play. If each customer service employee understands and plays their job character like the consummate actor, they will be more aware of what is really required to do their job.

In other words, I believe that great customer service is all an act! Not in a fake way. When an actor plays a role in which they have no direct experience, they draw on their personal experience to give their character life. The best actors are authentic, present, trusting and disciplined, attributes applicable to understanding the job character of all types of customer service professionals.

We have job descriptions and job specifications. I say we also need a job character profile — a "script" for the job character. This profile describes the goals, context, communication and behaviors of the job character, and provides guidance about how to "act" in the customer-service position.

Character goal. Helping the customer succeed and get what's needed. Every character in a play has a goal for his "journey," and the character's context, communication and behavior must advance that goal. The customer's goal is a beacon that guides the customer service employee.

Character context. How this character fits into the organization as a provider of customer service. If customer service is an afterthought in the organization, the customer service employee would serve only to fix problems, not anticipate them. But, if managing and growing customer relationships are important, the service professional will do whatever possible to help the customer succeed.

Character communication. The choice of words, expression of emotions, body language and use of silence must be carefully considered in the communication between service provider and customer.

Character behavior. Following through; being patient; offering options, suggestions and alternatives; paying attention; and really caring about the customer are tools the character uses.

Job character profiles can help individuals in customer positions know not just how and what to do in their jobs, but how and who to be in their jobs, which can lead to better overall "performances." And, it is certainly about time for this "act" to earn better reviews, wouldn't you agree?

LESSON MANTRA

My philosophy of customer service is built upon being authentic, fully present, disciplined and trusting.

PERSONAL NOTES:

QUESTIONS TO CONSIDER

Think of the worst customer experience you have ever had. Were you being reasonable in your expectations? Was the customer service provider being reasonable in their effort and commitment to meet your expectations?

What one thing – actions or words – would have prevented the problem from becoming so bad?

HOMEWORK

Regardless of your title, you provide "customer" service to someone – an external consumer, a supplier or vendor, or a co-worker in another department or division. Using your current position, write a one-page Job Character Profile. It should contain the following elements:

- Your job title
- The customer service *goal* of your specific job
- The customer service *context* your job has – for example, if you work as a staff accountant who provides financial information to other departments, your context is that others need and depend on you for accurate information to know how much more money they can or cannot spend
- The *communication* of your position as it relates to providing service. What words and tone you use, how do you use silence or

pauses, and how well you listen are all part of your communication.

- The final components to outline is your *behavior*. How you act – do you follow-through, do you stop yourself from getting defensive when someone is expressing an objection, how you show that you authentically care about the person to whom you are providing service – all of these factors and more define your behavior

It doesn't need to be anything fancy – but it does need to be written down and you need to post it somewhere it will be prominent and visible during your daily work as a reminder of who and how to be, not just what and how to do your job.

RESOURCES

American Customer Satisfaction Index. (2012). *ACSI Results.*
http://www.theacsi.org/index.php?option=com_content&view=article&id=12&Itemid=110

Butsunturn, C. (2012). Tepid rise in customer satisfaction mimics slow pace of economic recovery. *ACIS Index Press Releases.*
http://www.theacsi.org/index.php?option=com_content&view=article&id=275;press-release-february-2012&catid=14&Itemid=349

Contact Professional. (19 Oct 2011). Dissatisfied U.S. consumers becoming more vocal. *Contact Professional.*
http://www.contactprofessional.com/topics/customer-service-retention/news/dissatisfied-us-consumers-becoming-more-vocal-3224

Kaufman, R. (2009). Added value: In challenging time, service matters most. *GCI Magazine.* www.GCImagazine.com, 15-16.

Shehab, T. M., & Adler, L. A. (2009). The quest for service excellence – One group's journey. *Physician Executive,* 25(4): 40-45.

LESSON #7: Cultural competence or diversity dancing?

LESSON #7: Cultural competence or diversity dancing?

Is your company better at cultural competence or diversity dancing?

Since the 1980s, social anthropologists, sociologists and social workers have offered a variety of definitions of cultural competence. I prefer the one offered in the seminal 1989 work presented by the Georgetown University Child Development Center. In essence, cultural competence is a "set of congruent behaviors, attitudes and policies that come together" to facilitate effective work and productivity in multicultural contexts.

In addition, the work identified five elements that contribute to cultural competence: valuing diversity; being able to conduct cultural self-assessments; awareness of the dynamics of cultural interaction; institutionalized cultural knowledge; and adapting the way we do business to reflect our understanding of diversity.

I want to focus on valuing diversity.

I see a company's cultural competence as being good at working effectively on organization goals with employees who are different, with different defined as ethnicity, race, orientation, ability or gender. Today, cultural competence can be described as a continuum. The more culturally competent a company becomes, the further along the continuum it moves from tolerating diversity to celebrating diversity.

Here's an example.

Say XYZ Bank has a qualified African-American woman candidate for a position as marketing manager. A company with minimal cultural competence knows the law prohibits discrimination because of ethnicity, race and sex. In this case, the hiring bank says "I have to hire you" (tolerate diversity). The next stage acknowledges and includes people who are different in their hiring practices. It says, "I want to hire you" (accept diversity). Enthusiastically embracing human differences is the final stage, the most culturally competent. In this case, the bank says, "I'd love to hire you!" (celebrate diversity).

Ideally, companies want to strive toward the "love to hire you" stage, where the differences an individual brings not only are acknowledged and accepted, but sought after as a valuable asset.

The best characterization of celebrating diversity was articulated by Shirley Chisholm, a seven-term member of the U.S. House of Representatives from New York and the first black woman elected to Congress. I heard her speak years ago at a public housing conference. Of the "melting pot" metaphor, Chisholm said: "We are nobody's melting pot! We are a beautiful, giant salad bowl." And, she went on to describe that the best salads were made of ingredients that varied in texture, taste, color and size: lettuce, onions, croutons, tomatoes, peppers, dressing. Her metaphor has stuck with me to this day.

What about diversity dancing? In my opinion, a result of the well-intended, albeit misunderstood, cultural sensitivity training and education we have imposed on our employees is that we have made the Archie Bunkers of the world (or those like Stan Smith in "American Dad," for the under-35 set) bad and wrong and unwittingly created a culture of diversity dancers. The diversity dancers are those closeted Bunkers and Smiths who have learned the dance steps of political correctness while continuing to harbor bigotry and disdain. It's kind of like slipping on that banana peel while you're trying to dance.

Let me be clear about one thing. As someone who conducts diversity training, I think that cultural training and education is necessary and important. The problem is that too often the training intellectualizes the issue rather than hits the heart of the matter — and I mean that literally. Diversity is processed in the heart, not the head. Until an individual feels what it is like to be excluded, demeaned or hurt because he is different, he just doesn't get it. And when that same individual is wanted, recruited, welcomed and enjoyed because he is different, he does get it.

What can companies do to move toward more cultural competence? It strikes me as funny in a sad sort of way that we expect our employees to accept and celebrate diversity of people, yet we frequently seem so intolerant of diversity of thought. So maybe the first step is celebrating different ideas rather than shooting them down as "we tried that" or "that'll never work."

Then, we can help our employees get to know one another in a nonworking social context, like a day of community service. It's amazing how difficult it is to despise or fear someone you know more personally.

Third, encourage employees to talk about their feelings about diversity. I know this is the social worker in me, but it is OK for employees to discuss feelings. It doesn't have to become like the free-for-all, touchy-feely T-groups of the '70s. With structured and effective facilitation, talking about feelings can identify stories that are untrue, or at least not always true, and build bridges where there are gaps in understanding.

Finally, be honest about where your company is right now on the continuum, so you can develop a realistic and attainable plan for where you want to go.

So, are you ready to answer the question, or are you too busy dancing?

LESSON MANTRA

I believe that proactively including and authentically valuing culturally diversity among employees, customers and stakeholders is the right and profitable strategy for success.

PERSONAL NOTES:

QUESTIONS TO CONSIDER

How are you different from everyone else in your workplace? Diversity extends beyond race, gender, orientation and the more obvious differences. Being hearing impaired, ADD, introverted among a group of extroverts, or left-handed contributes to our individuality and diversity.

Recall the last time your "diversity" was used against you or you felt disempowered because you are different. What was the impact of this experience on your productivity, self-esteem or mood? What would have made this situation less unpleasant or prevented it from happening?

HOMEWORK

Pick an aspect of human diversity about which you have the least knowledge or experience. For example, if you have no gay family members or friends, pick homosexuality; if you don't know anyone with a learning disability, pick one of the learning disabilities; or, if you have no experience with people who have substance addictions (i.e. drugs, alcohol, etc.), pick one of those. The point here is to select something that you're intimidated by, ignorant of, or have strong opinions about.

Now that you have an area of diversity, Google® it. But, before you do that, make one promise – that you will take on this assignment openly, purging your mind of all preconceived notions and assumptions.
After you have done your "research," write down (yes, it's important that you write it down), at least 5 things that you didn't know, found out you didn't know completely accurately, or had it all wrong.

I need you to make another promise. This time, promise that you will use what you learned from identifying your Top 5 to guide how you treat, behave, and think the next time you are faced with dealing with any type of human diversity (not limited to your specific Top 5) with which you are not family or comfortable.

RESOURCES

20th Century Fox Television, Atlantic Creative, Fuzzy Door Productions, & Underdog Productions. (Producer). (2005). *American Dad*. Los Angeles: Fox.

Cross, T. L., Bazron, B. J., Dennis, K. W., & Isaacs, M. R. (1989). *Towards a culturally competent system of care: a monograph on effective services for minority children who are severely emotionally disturbed*. Washington, DC: CASSP Technical Assistance Center.

Edmundson, P. J. (2005). Preparing culturally competent leaders. *The New York Times*. http://www.nytimes.com/ref/college/coll-opinion-edmundson.html

Fishman, C. (25 October 1992). Shirley Chisholm: the pioneering congresswoman, on the melting pot 'myth' and moving to Florida. *Orlando Sentinel*. http://articles.orlandosentinel.com/1992-10-25/news/9211041135_1_shirley-chisholm-dirty-politics-posture

Triandis, H. C., Kurowski, L. L., & Gelfand, M. J. (1994). Workplace diversity. *Handbook of industrial and organizational psychology, 4*, 769-827.

LESSON #8: Women leaders – essential to productivity.

LESSON #8: Women leaders – essential to productivity.

In our previous lesson, we talked about the diversity dance that some companies do around the issues of race, gender, sexual orientation, religion and ability. To me, that dance is never more alive than with issues of women in the workplace. There are so many important aspects to this topic: pay equity, harassment, work/life balance, the glass ceiling.

But there's one in particular to which I'd like to give voice: valuing women's ways of managing and leading.

For years, the accepted way for men to manage and lead in the workplace was the "command-and-control" style. It was "comfortable" for men because their power to command/control comes from positions of leadership and authority. In command-and-control, one does what one is asked (or told), no questions asked, and is rewarded accordingly.

Not so for women in similar positions. As women's presence in visible organizational positions grew in the 1980s and '90s, their style of leading and managing was considered by their male counterparts to be feminine and inappropriate. Judy B. Rosener, in her 2000 Harvard Business Review article, "Ways Women Lead," summarized the context best. She described how the lack of "authority over others and control over resources" in the workplace forced women to rely on what came naturally or what was socially accepted. Their power comes from personality, interpersonal skills, diligence and networking. According to Rosener, the style includes encouraging participation, sharing information and power, enhancing self-worth and energizing others.

Before I get too far, let me acknowledge that a certain amount of stereotyping serves as the basis for her premise and my opinions that follow. But, that is not a reason to discount either.

Rosener and other management intellectuals described the difference as transactional versus transformational. Men are more likely to characterize their relationship with subordinates as exchanging rewards for services rendered or punishment for poor performance. Women, on the other hand, talk of getting subordinates to transform their own self-interest and align it with organizational interests and goals.

So that's the framework for understanding basic differences in style. Here is some of what women add because of the way they manage and lead.

Facilitation. Instead of "running" meetings, groups and processes, women have taught us more about how to facilitate them. Facilitation engages participants. Setting agenda, creating strategy, implementing plans and evaluating practices are achieved by including and involving participants, not merely telling them what is going to happen and what they are going to do.

Managing affect. Stereotypical "good 'ol boy" managers would have you think that acknowledging and expressing feelings in the workplace is a sign of weakness for wimps or whiners. But, despite the reliance on technology, organizations still make products and deliver services through people – living, feeling beings. Female leaders and managers have shown us how to manage feelings in a way that leave employees feeling respected, heard and valued. A concept called emotional intelligence, which is all about managing affect, now has credibility in today's workplace.

Real listening. You know the difference. The "listener" who nods frequently and utters "ah-huh, ah-huh" but is only humoring you so you'll finish so they can say what he wants to say. Let's face it, women have not only been socialized to listen, but we expect to be heard when we vent or complain to them. Empathizing can clear away obstacles to productivity and quality and set the stage for passion and loyalty.

Transparency. Since women in the workplace initially couldn't get behind the proverbial closed doors where the dealmakers were, they made their deals in the open. It's not a coincidence to me that the three people who pulled the plug on the covert, illegal shenanigans going on at WorldCom, Enron and the FBI back in 2002 were all women.

Mentoring. Women are socialized to be the nurturers. So, when women were excluded from the links or the happy-hour drinks, they sought their own nurturing and support informally by talking with one another, or by creating support groups in the workplace. Today, mentoring programs are common in business.

Excitement and fun. I think one outcome from women energizing others is that the workplace is more exciting and more fun, or at least more relaxed. This does not have to mean it's less competitive or industrious. I think even men will agree with me that we have come to realize that working hard doesn't have to be drudgery or unpleasant. No wonder we needed so many happy hours!

The bottom line: Women in the workplace have been great for business. Women have taught us a lot about organizational effectiveness because they are always mindful that the most important resources we manage and lead at work are people.

Women work well in business. Organizations need to make it okay for women to stop the "dance" they have had to do to be effective, so they can do their job and make even greater contributions to the world of work.

LESSON MANTRA

I celebrate the contributions and competencies of the leaders who are women.

PERSONAL NOTES:

QUESTIONS TO CONSIDER

What contributions have you made (as a woman) or observed women make to your workplace? Were they acknowledged in the same way as similar ones made by men in your workplace? If not, why?

What can you do to elevate the status and respect for the contributions made by women in your workplace?

HOMEWORK

The first step in this assignment is to acknowledge that you have an "inner woman leader" inside – regardless of your gender. In some cases, the woman leader is stifled, devalued or even dismissed. That ends now. From this moment forward, you will embrace your inner woman leader.

Next, select one of the competencies I describe above that women add to the workplace as managers and leaders. Your choices include: facilitation, managing effect, real listening, transparency, mentoring, excitement and fun. Ideally, you pick the one about which you feel the least competent.

So, with an inner woman competency identified, your task now is to become fully present (conscious) to the competency and create opportunities to practice it. For example, if real listening has not been one of your strengths when dealing with your co-workers, make it your "mission" to develop your listening – authentic, empathic listening . To do this will mean you may have to do some research on what real listening entails. I can tell you that it means putting all of your attention on the speaker, rather than you the listener. It means being able to feedback what exactly was said, minus any filtering we do consciously or unconsciously.

And, finally, it means acknowledging and empathizing with the message and the speaker, and acting accordingly.

Don't think that there has to be some major crisis or problem for you to practice your newly recognized competency. It's in the everyday, routine practices of our work where through which we grow and become great.

RESOURCES

Blum, T. C., Fields, D. L., & Goodman, J. S. (1994). Organization-level determinants of women in management. *Academy of Management Journal,* 37(2) 241-68.

Jogulu, U. D., & Wood, G. J. (2006). The role of leadership theory in raising the profile of women in management. *Equal Opportunities International,* 25(4), 236-50.

Rosener, J. B. (1990). Ways women lead. *Harvard Business Review,* 68(6), 119-25.

Wilen-Daugenti, T. (2013). How women's leadership shines in the workplace. *Examiner.com.* http://www.examiner.com/article/how-women-s-leadership-shines-the-workplace

LESSON #9: The case for sabbaticals.

LESSON #9: The case for sabbaticals.

In preparing for this lesson, I learned that the term "sabbatical" has historical biblical roots to *shmita*, the Jewish commandment to "let land lie fallow (unplanted) once every seven years," as in "And, on the seventh day He rested."

I didn't know that.

And I just finished my second sabbatical from my work at Moravian College.

Whether you take it from the Latin, Greek or Hebrew, a sabbatical is literally a "ceasing." It has come to be known as a leave (often some portion of it is paid) from one's career for the purpose of achieving a specific professional goal, such as writing a book. What it has come to mean to many of my friends, is a year or a semester off for college professors.

For me that couldn't be further from the truth. During my first sabbatical, I developed and tested a program for orienting new board members of not-for-profit organizations. This time, I created a training program for customer service personnel that uses theater as its basis. In both sabbaticals, I was relieved from my teaching, advising and committee responsibilities, but in addition to those projects above, I took on a variety of community leadership and service projects as well.

The bottom line: I ramped up my activities, albeit at a more casual pace and flexible timeline. The result: a recharged battery that energizes my passion for teaching and writing. I can honestly say that I enjoy teaching today as much or more (depending on the day) as I did the first time I walked into a college classroom as a 24-year-old instructor.

So are the benefits of sabbaticals reserved for the ivory tower dwellers, or might these benefits be applicable to many business and organization contexts?

CNNMoney claims that nearly 25 percent of the companies listed in the 100 Best Companies to Work For in 2012 offer paid sabbaticals. And the Society of Human Resource Management for its 2011 Benefits Report surveyed approximately 600 employers, mostly in the U.S. The report found 15 percent offer paid sabbatical programs, while an additional 4 percent offer unpaid sabbatical programs as a benefit to their employees. That's about 1 in 5 employers.

McDonald's, the golden-arched colossus, gives every salaried employee eight weeks paid leave for every 10 years of employment, a practice they've done for the past 40 years.

Paid leaves seem to be gaining in popularity. But not surprisingly, a benefit has to make cents, as well as sense.

In a 2006 article, Bloomberg BusinessWeek reported the biggest obstacles that prevent employers from offering sabbaticals are the obvious ones: money and time. Sabbaticals cost the company money, and finding someone to do the work in the person's absence can be a challenge.

But this article also said that many human resource managers believe the benefits outweigh the costs. They outlined at least six of the most significant pro-sabbatical reasons.

First, giving employees a periodic respite is a much-needed break from always having to be "on" or "connected." Second, the expense of sabbaticals is often more than recouped in reduced turnover (reason No. 3) and retained wisdom otherwise lost when veteran employees burn out (No. 4).

And when they come back, the employees return more committed and more energized (No. 5), and more likely to stay with the company. Finally, sabbaticals give managers a chance to see how well others perform and step up while filling in for their colleagues.

Of course, the success of sabbaticals hinges on two critical components. First, there needs to be a clear understanding between employer and employee regarding expectations. What exactly is agreed to be the "outcome" of the sabbatical? Will the employee create, develop or complete a project, or will they commit to disconnecting from their responsibilities and frenetic pace, and reconnect with their soul and spirit? Both are equally valid.

Second, the sabbatical employee must show integrity. The employee needs to do what he or she promised while on sabbatical, whether it's the project or the mental break.

I know what you might be thinking: No way can I afford to pay any of my employees to take off three months or more for a sabbatical.

Hear me out.

Allowing employees to develop a project, work from home or create a new business for your business can achieve similar sabbatical-like benefits. It might be as simple as allowing employees to have free time during the day to daydream. Consider that what may appear to be an unproductive use of time now might actually morph into a lucrative competitive advantage for your company in the future. And a sabbatical in any form might be another way to infuse passion into your workplace.

I get your concern that some people may abuse the benefit. But just as it is in academia, in business it should be that if you have no integrity (fail to do what you promised) during one sabbatical, your chances of getting another one are bleak. If you are smart about this – have a carefully crafted application and selection process, and have clear expectations about outcomes – a sabbatical program can become something that your employees will want to work for. And for those who receive it, it will be a reminder of the confidence you have and investment you are making in them.

Embrace the sabbatical, because we all deserve to rest on the seventh day.

LESSON MANTRA

I will adopt a sabbatical mentality – even if I can't take the time off, I will take a break!

PERSONAL NOTES:

QUESTIONS TO CONSIDER

If you were given a sabbatical from your employer, what would you do with your time away from the job?

How would this sabbatical benefit - you as a person? As an employee? Your company?

What would make it possible for your employer to offer you a sabbatical?

HOMEWORK

Unfortunately, I can't guarantee your employee will give you a sabbatical or even that she or he won't laugh you out of their office at the mere mention of one; however, I can help you claim at least one of the benefits that sabbaticals can provide: detachment from daily routine, otherwise known as a break.

To tap in to the sabbatical "break," you need to be willing to untether yourself from at least some of the daily routines of a demanding work life. For example, having your email come directly to your phone is convenient but can prevent you from taking a healthy "break" from work.

So, I want you to select the aspect of your work life around which you are most obsessed. For me, it is check email. I have all my emails (7 separate addresses) all accessible on my phone. I have been able to stop myself from immediately (as in, the second the email messages arrive) responding. My new guideline is to respond in the same day, just not the same hour. Now, let's be clear – I'm not suggesting you slack off on your communication or responsibilities. I am suggesting that you self-monitor an area that is particularly an obstacle to having some reasonable "break" from the daily demands of our work life. Give it a try. It will be awkward and perhaps even a little stressful at first, but, in the longer-term, it will help you take a much-deserved break.

RESOURCES

100 best companies to work for. (6 February 2012). *Fortune Magazine.*
http://money.cnn.com/magazines/fortune/best-companies/

Arndt, M. (8 January 2006). Nice work if you can get it. *Bloomberg BusinessWeek.* http://www.businessweek.com/stories/2006-01-08/nice-work-if-you-can-get-it

Kennedy, K., & Malveaux, J. (2011). *2011 employee benefits, examining employee benefits amidst uncertainty.* Society for Human Resource Management: http://www.shrm.org/research/surveyfindings/articles/documents/2011_emp_benefits_report.pdf

Sima, C. M. (2000). The role and benefits of the sabbatical leave in faculty development and satisfaction. *New Directions for Institutional Research.* 2000(105). 67-75.

LESSON #10: So you want to buy some cookies, right?

LESSON #10: So you want to buy some cookies, right?

If your company is going to allow Girls Scout Cookie sales and other office fundraisers, it's a good idea to develop a set of ground rules so that solicitations don't cause problems.

At least once a year, it's a special time when some very big decisions will be made. Debt reduction and sequestration? Privatize the lottery? Nah. I'm talking about the choice between Thin Mints or Trefoils, Tagalongs or Do-Si-Dos – which is a pretty good indication that it's Girl Scout Cookie® season. And, since that isn't the only time of year our work colleagues are hawking their kids' fundraisers, I thought it would be a good idea to present this lesson: how to handle solicitations in the workplace.

Now, let's begin with an important disclaimer: Charitable campaigns and projects are good. Getting employees engaged in charitable activities is an excellent way to demonstrate good corporate social responsibility and care for the community by supporting the many worthy not-for-profit organizations (NFPs). But, as with anything, there's an appropriate and inappropriate way that this can be done.

Let's look at some examples.

"Buy my daughter's troop cookies and you can have the afternoon off."

"If you don't order my son's Little League hoagie, you can forget about that promotion."

"Our company supports the Everyone's Gotta Read Foundation, so you will be volunteering as a tutor once a week."

Obviously, these are extreme examples, but they do fairly represent what happens in the workplace and why solicitations at work could be problematic. Harassment, abuses of power or position, coercion and unfair treatment can result if solicitation is not managed.

Here's how I see the problems playing out:

Harassment: Aggressive, intrusive or repeated attempts to get you to participate in community or charitable projects, even if your company approves a charitable activity, can be harassing behavior.

Abuse of position or authority: If your boss is the solicitor, chances are that she may not perceive what she's doing as taking advantage of the power she has. So, here's a simple test: How easy or hard is it to say no? In other words, if there is a reward or consequence, however slight, attached to your participation or lack thereof, the boss likely is overstepping boundaries of professionalism.

Coercion: Even when the boss is not the solicitor, coercion can be the primary tactic used. No matter how friendly, approaches that in essence, force, intimidate or compel the employee to participate are inappropriate and demeaning.

Inconsistent practices: You may not realize this, but permitting solicitations, even charitable ones, may create problems if unions are not allowed to distribute literature or recruit in your workplace.

Keeping track of participation: Documenting who gives or doesn't give, or how much they give, might be used against an employee. This information could be used against a person in terms of future performance evaluations, raises, promotions or just being included or not included in the work community.

In these cases, doing good will be bad for the company or organization. They will probably hurt morale, productivity and community within the company. Avoid them; the possible benefits are not worth the cost.

My suggestion? Have and enforce a solicitations policy with the following components:

- Allow only charitable activities approved by the company or organization that solicits money, volunteers or support.

- Prohibit solicitations of employees or volunteers in work areas (space owned or leased by the company) of any type by nonemployees.
- The policy includes all employees and volunteers.
- Solicitation is only permitted during non-work time, such as lunch period or breaks.
- Use of company or organization resources such as a copy machine, postage and email to solicit employees or volunteers is prohibited, unless the solicitation is approved by the company.
- Consider any National Labor Relations Board regulations that may apply to your company in creating a solicitation policy.
- Do not keep records of individual participation. Documenting total participation for aggregate reporting (as in, say, 75 percent of the organization's employees contributed to a Hurricane Sandy Relief Campaign) is OK, and important data to maintain.

Want a bottom-line rule of thumb?

For the company-sanctioned drives: Use the charitable activity to build employee morale, community support and social responsibility, making sure you don't alienate or treat employees unfairly. For the everyday, non-company-sanctioned charitable drives: Allow employees and volunteers to send one email to co-workers that announces the charitable activity in which they are involved and tells co-workers how they can participate, should they choose to.

So, those big decisions?

I'll go with a balance of spending cuts and some additional new revenue, and two boxes of Trefoils. Just don't bring them to my office.

LESSON MANTRA

I will encourage participation and support for charitable initiatives at work without imposing it.

PERSONAL NOTES:

QUESTIONS TO CONSIDER

Have you been "solicited" at work (not that type of solicitation, that's covered in Lesson #12)? By whom? Your boss? Co-worker? What did you do? Why?

If you have solicited your co-workers, were you low-pressure and easy going or a pain in the butt?

In either case – as a solicitor or a "solicitee" – was the outcome positive? In answering this question, don't just consider if you made or exceeded your goal. Consider if people don't walk (run?) in the other direction when they see you heading their way.

HOMEWORK

Select a social issue or charitable cause for which you have a passion and commitment to make a difference. Is there an existing campaign or activity that already exists to promote the issue or cause? If so, talk with your company about if and how you and your employer could offer support. If not, create a way to increase visibility about the issue or cause among your company and co-workers.

Neither has to be a time-consuming or labor-intensive initiative. Simply having a face-to-face, sending an email message, or bringing the issue up at a staff meeting may be enough to make a difference among your co-workers perceptions or understanding of the issue.

You're not trying to raise a million dollars, just raise awareness and interest.

RESOURCES

Davis, C. T. (2010). Solicitation and distribution: who can do what, when and where? *Ogletree Deakins.*
http://www.ogletreedeakins.com/publications/2010-04-26/solicitation-and-distribution-who-can-do-what-when-and-where

Humphries, A. (2000, December 21). *What the dickens?* (Porter Anderson, Interviewer).
http://edition.cnn.com/2000/CAREER/corporateclass/12/21/charity/

Rubin, J. W., Berkowitz, A. D., & Hoffman, J. A. (2009). Solicitation and
distribution policies under the national labor relations act: a guide to
current compliance and anticipated future developments. *Bloomberg Law
Reports.* http://www.dechert.com/files/Publication/7f096ace-88f4-4f46-
9a9b-45c51f656342/Presentation/PublicationAttachment/d35ab41e-
249d-4cce-bd11-
4ed266b0d934/solicitation%20and%20distribution%20policies%20under
%20the%20national%20labor%20relations%20act.pdf

Selling or soliciting on work time. (2013). *U.S. Chamber of Commerce Small
Business Nation.*
http://www.uschambersmallbusinessnation.com/toolkits/guide/P05_5410

LESSON #11: Mixing work and romance are rarely a good idea.

LESSON #11: Mixing work and romance are rarely a good idea.

Can romance and professionalism coexist in the workplace?

It's a relationship cliché: Put two people in the same office, add some mutual attraction and a little friendly flirting. And pretty soon, it's a match – better than any online dating site, right?

Well, I wouldn't hire the DJ and rent the hall just yet.

But despite all the uncertainty and potential red flags, this situation is pretty common. Career websites such as CareerBuilder.com and Vault.com put the number at somewhere between 38 percent and 59 percent. That's the percentage of workers who have dated a colleague at least one time during their career, with nearly a third of them marrying the person they dated at work.

While many may find love at work, very few actually make love there. According to a Bloomburg BusinessWeek report, less than 5 percent of sexual encounters happen at work. But there are good reasons that sex in the office is less common than romance in the office.

Most people who have sex in the office get caught. Research shows that if you communicated any evidence of your "activities" – via email, text, IM – you are likely to be, pardon the expression, exposed.

And if that happens, be ready for the consequences. At the very least, you can expect to be the subject of office gossip, or worse, Twitter gossip (Twossip?).

In addition, your reputation for professionalism may be forever suspect. Worst case, one of you may be forced to find another job.

To be clear: Don't date at work! Don't have sex in the office!

That said, I get that dating at work might be unavoidable. You can't help who you are attracted to. But you can help how you act. So if the chemistry is just so overpowering, and you don't have enough challenges to deal with, and you must mix personal and professional, then do yourself and your company a favor and follow these Office Dating Do's and Don'ts:

- Do know and respect company policy on dating. Violations could lead to disciplinary action or even termination.
- Don't date someone you supervise or who supervises you. But if you're really a glutton for punishment and you do, take Forbes suggestion and sign a "cupid contract" that is filed with HR and spells out the mutual agreements in case things don't work out.

- Do think ahead. What happens if the relationship fizzles or ends badly? Are you prepared for the scornful looks from your ex's sympathetic co-workers?

- Don't date someone who is married or in a relationship, no matter how many fantasies it might fulfill.

- Don't flirt. It's not cute, and it's certainly not the same as being friendly; you know the difference. Flirting could unwittingly send unintended messages.

- Do control yourself. Act professionally. Your co-workers didn't sign up for front-row seats to "Days of Your Lives."

- Don't blab or brag. This includes through email, IMs, phone calls, the "promise you won't tell" conversations and Happy Hour buzzes.

This lesson's bottom line: *Don't do it.* But if you can't avoid it, be smart about it. And while this lesson has been mostly directed to employees, here's a tip for companies: Be clear about what is permitted in the way of personal relationships, document it as an explicit policy in your employee handbook or personnel policy manual, and hold everyone (CEOs, in particular) accountable to it.

To answer my original question: Can romance and professionalism coexist in the workplace? I'd have to give an unenthusiastic "possibly," but it requires a lot of work to do it well.

LESSON MANTRA

I am an adult who knows and respects personal boundaries at work. If I cross them or they become blurred, I will behave responsibly and professionally, in ways that would make my mother proud!

PERSONAL NOTES:

QUESTIONS TO CONSIDER

Have you ever been involved with a romantic or sexual relationship at work? (Remember, no one knows your answers, so be honest). If so, do you have any regrets? If yes, what are they?

Do you think it's unrealistic or naïve to expect employees to avoid dating at work, or is it just part of being a professional?

HOMEWORK

If you are married, skip this homework assignment; if single, read on and get out your notepad cuz it's time to write a little story.

First, identify (only to yourself) the person in your company with whom - if given the right opportunity, situations and alignment of the moon and the stars – you would be interested in a romantic relationship.

Next, follow the scenario through – start with the flirting and the excitement, to the dating and the physical and emotional connections, to the end. Yes, consider what it would be like if the relationship ended, in the worst, possible way. How would it be for you, and how do you imagine it would be for the other person, at work? If you're still up for dating at work, then you have my best wishes and let me know where you're registered for the wedding!

RESOURCES

Cohen, A. (12 November, 2012). How often do people have sex at the office? *Bloomberg BusinessWeek.* http://www.businessweek.com/articles/2012-11-12/how-often-do-people-have-sex-at-the-office

Grasz, J. (2013). Three in ten workers who had office romances married their co-worker, finds annual CareerBuilder Valentine's Day survey. *Careerbuilder.com.* http://www.careerbuilder.com/share/aboutus/pressreleasesdetail.aspx?sd=2/13/2013&id=pr40&ed=12/31/2013

Schawbel, D. (2012). Why you should stay away from office romances. *Forbes.* http://www.forbes.com/sites/danschawbel/2012/01/13/why-you-should-stay-away-from-office-romances/

Vandewater, C. (14 February 2012). In defense of office romance. *Vault.com.* http://blogs.vault.com/blog/workplace-issues/in-defense-of-office-romance/

LESSON #12: Loafing on the Job, the Cyber Way!

LESSON #12: Loafing on the Job, the Cyber Way!

Loaf – to spend time in idleness, to sleep, perchance to dream (sorry!). I remember working as a stock clerk/cashier at a supermarket in high school and college. There were "certain people" (not I, of course) who had a reputation as a "load" – as in someone who loafed and did whatever they could to avoid working. Today, thanks to modern technology and the Internet, that title has morphed into cyber-loafing. The meaning's still the same, but the method has gotten an upgrade.

A study by a Kansas State University researcher found that between 60 and 80 percent of the time employees spend on the Internet at work has nothing to do with their job. They coined the term cyber-loafing. Their study found that loafing transcends age, but younger people loaf to socialize, while older employees are more interested in more pragmatic activities such as managing their finances.

In any case, LearnStuff.com estimates the cost to productivity is more than $650 billion dollars. To combat the drain on productivity, many companies have resorted to three major strategies: monitor computer use by employees; establish policies that restrict use; and, publicize the consequences for employees who cyber-loaf.

Let's take a look at each strategy. First, monitoring computer use. Big Employer is watching. And, while it has the right to, is it really a helpful tactic to perpetuate a nurturing work culture? Will watching employees' every keystroke (there are programs that do this) build and sustain trust among employees that is so desperately needed to be productive and effective? I doubt it. In fact, I think it creates a game of "catch-me-if-you-can," which is even a greater drain on productivity.

How about establishing policies to restrict computer use? According to Salary.com, about 30 percent of employees surveyed report that their employers are doing just that. I agree that a policy is a good idea, but only a Band-Aid for what may really be going on. Before establishing a policy, I suggest you delve a bit into knowing why are your employees cyber-loafing to begin with? Are they un-motivated, under-challenged? It would seem to me that if employees had enough meaningful work, they might be more passionate about their job and have less time or desire to disconnect from their job in a cyber-way.

The third strategy – publicizing the punishment – is simply ludicrous if you aspire to treat your employees as mature adults who are prepared to work hard in return for fair treatment and compensation. Yes, it should be made clear what the consequences of violating the policy are, but I don't think you want to post the offenses on your company's Facebook page.

So what's a company or not-for-profit organization to do?

First, assess, rather than monitor, your employees' cyber activities. As I mentioned above, it's important to understand why your employees are cyber-loafing. Determine if possible, if it is a trend or an isolated incident among a select number of employees. The more you know about why and how frequently this is happening, the more effective you'll be a creating a solution.

Second, understand the difference between cyber-loafing and productive, even if not directly related, use of the Internet at work. Cyber-loafing will more likely be found among employees whose work ethic shows other signs of carelessness or indifference. Star or committed employees' cyber-activities are not likely to be loafing, even if it looks that way. A study by the University of Melbourne (Australia) found that limited non-work related cyber-activities increased productivity by 9 percent. In their research, the productivity increase occurred for 70 percent of people permitted to "play" on the Internet (i.e. watch videos, use social media, etc.) for 20 percent of their workday. In short, if you are focusing on employee performance – both productivity (quantity) and effectiveness (quality) - cyber-activities of employees who are loafing will be very distinguishable from those activities which may be beneficial. This leads to my next point.

Third, acknowledge and leverage the many potential benefits of employees' cyber activities. When your employees are "present" (visible and active) on the Internet, there is the potential for them to be more knowledgeable, informed and aware, about issues that are directly or indirectly relevant to their job or your company. This enhanced awareness may help them and you solve problems or create solutions to challenges you face. Finally, being "connected" can help them sell your company and your product, or at least create a positive "buzz" about them.

Fourth, establish a policy that is clear and firm on the following points:

- Approach the issue from the assumption that cyber activities of employees can enhance their performance productivity and effectiveness

- Prohibit illegal and inappropriate (you determine what that is, based on your company culture) cyber activities

- Communicate that it is not okay to text, surf or cyber-loaf at meetings, in discussions with co-workers or any customer interactions

- Enumerate the consequences of violating the policy; consequences of varying degrees of disciplinary action, including termination, may be warranted if that is consistent with the offense and your disciplinary approach in general

Employees: I know you don't want to be a "load" so be reasonable about how and when you engage in cyber-activities at work. Show your boss that you can still be an excellent worker and that your Internet activities can actually help you do your job or improve the company.

with your organization. Don't expect to get a raise or promotion, but you might just get some kudos for looking out for the best interests of your company.

For example, a volunteer coordinator for a NFP organization who is surfing the Internet for a gift for their significant other, might come across a gift idea for recognizing outstanding volunteers at the annual meeting; or, a bank teller investigating CD rates for their personal investments might come across an appealing marketing strategy used by another financial services company that could be considered for getting customers to open deposit accounts.

RESOURCES

Magid, L. (3 April 2009). Study: 'leisure browsing' increases productivity. *C/Net.* http://news.cnet.com/8301-19518_3-10211019-238.html

Social media at work. (26 October 2012). LearnStuff.com. http://www.learnstuff.com/social-media-at-work/

Study: Americans spend up to 80 percent of internet time 'cyberloafing.' (5 February 2013). CBS-St. Louis. http://stlouis.cbslocal.com/2013/02/05/study-americans-spend-up-to-80-percent-of-work-time-cyberloafing/

Why & how your employees are wasting time at work. (2012). Salary.com. http://business.salary.com/why-how-your-employees-are-wasting-time-at-work/

Lesson #13: Being "good" at bearing bad news.

Lesson #13: Being "good" at bearing bad news.

Hopefully, you've only experienced the sting of that decree vicariously through the losers of reality TV's "The Apprentice." But I'm sure many of you have probably received or had to deliver some sort of bad news at work, from telling someone they didn't get the promotion to telling your boss you didn't meet your quarterly sales goals. Here are some suggestions on how to be good at delivering bad news.

Even with unemployment lingering at 7 percent, job losses are still an all-too-common occurrence for many workplaces. A 2010 report by the Heritage Foundation shows that manufacturing employment has fallen by one-third in the past decade. And that's while productivity went up. Job losses and increased efficiencies have been driven by technological innovation and improvements.

Thanks to technology, the company you run is becoming more efficient, more productive, and that makes your products more affordable to consumers. That's the good news.

And, you don't need as many people to do that. And that's still good news for you; but, not necessarily for some of your employees.

For many companies, it's an awkward place to be.

So, how can we be good bearers of bad news? Well, there are a few things not to do.

Don't delay. Avoiding the inevitable is just that. The delay often creates more opportunity for increased tension, stress and morale problems. And while the element of surprise might be a fun way to celebrate a birthday, it's a terrible way to tell someone they lost their job.

Don't hide. By far the worst thing you can do is to hide behind a phone, an email or a text to let someone know they have been fired. Amazingly, well-established organizations, who should know better, have been guilty of this. In 2006, RadioShack fired more than 400 people by email. In 2011, former Yahoo CEO Carol Bartz and Penn State coaching legend Joe Paterno both were fired by telephone. It is a cowardly and disrespectful way to terminate an employee, regardless of their performance, but especially if their job loss is motivated by economic conditions. And, no, Skype is not any better.

OK, so there's no easy way to deal with bad news. Being a manager requires a strength and integrity of character that seems to have been lost. I have no data to back this up, but my hunch is that many people currently in positions of management do not fully grasp or embody the character one must take on to effectively communicate bad news.

Harsh? Maybe. But I'm hopeful that with encouragement and coaching, we can be better. Here are some ideas to keep in mind.

First, it's not about you. If you think it's difficult to be the bearer of bad news, imagine what it's like to receive it. Take the focus you have on your insecurities and discomfort, and place that attention on empathy (not sympathy) for the person or group to whom you need to communicate this message.

Second, acknowledge that this is serious stuff. Whether it is a job loss or any other type of negative message, think and act with the careful and thoughtful attention such a situation deserves. This means you need to develop a plan for communicating the news. This is not a time to practice your "think-on-your-feet" skills.

Third, when necessary, take action early as possible. If a financial situation or individual performance makes it clear that terminating an employee or not promoting him is the right path to take, then communicate this sooner rather than later. For your company and your employee's sake, deal with it now.

Fourth, deliver the news in person. I cannot think of one instance where a direct supervisor can legitimately claim anything but face to face as an appropriate means for communicating bad news. And that includes virtual supervisors based in another state or country. Fly in if you have to. It will make the world of difference to your employees.

Fifth, be clear and compassionate. Leave no doubts or false hopes, but be the trustee of the individual's dignity and respect. In your message, include gratitude for the employee's contributions. Everyone makes some positive contribution.

Last, but definitely not least, offer support. Whether it is outplacement services, for those let go due to economic conditions, or help with collecting their personal belongings and having closure, do what you can to ease the sting. Most support costs a company nothing but means everything to your employee.

I stayed away from legal issues here, because I'm not an attorney. Follow the law, and protect yourself and your company, but protect and care for your employee, too.

If you have to be the one who has to say "You're fired," do it with as much grace and good judgment as you use to hire and manage.

LESSON MANTRA

I will always remember to separate the message from the person, and that even when the news is bad, the employee never is.

PERSONAL NOTES:

QUESTIONS TO CONSIDER

What was the "worst" news you received at work? What was the "worst" news you had to deliver at work? In either case, was it delivered well? Why?

What is your preferred way to receive "bad" news? To deliver it?

What do you think is the biggest obstacle to being "good" at bearing "bad" news?

HOMEWORK

The chances are great that if you haven't already, you will be faced with being the person to bear bad news.

Remember the trusted screener from Lesson 5. Well, you may want to recall them for this assignment (or at least someone with similar characteristics – that is, someone you trust and who will be honest). In this assignment, the trusted screener becomes the trusted receiver… of the bad news.

Pick a topic as your "bad news" to deliver – firing, demoting, not getting a promotion or raise, not accepting a proposal or idea. Practice telling your trusted receiver that bad news. Role-play with them where, how and what you would communicate. Ask them for their candid and critical feedback on how your communication impacted them and what you might do differently to be better at bearing bad news.

RESOURCES

Bies, R. (30 May 2012). The 10 commandments of for delivering bad news. *Forbes.*

http://www.forbes.com/sites/forbesleadershipforum/2012/05/30/10-commandments-for-delivering-bad-news/

RadioShack lays off employees via e-mail. (2 March, 2007). *USA Today.*

http://usatoday30.usatoday.com/tech/news/2006-08-30-radioshack-email-layoffs_x.htm?csp=34

Sherk, J. (12 October 2010). Technology explains drop in manufacturing jobs. *The Heritage Foundation.*

http://www.heritage.org/research/reports/2010/10/technology-explains-drop-in-manufacturing-jobs

Suddath, C. (9 May 2013). The right way for a CEO to deliver bad news. *Bloomberg BusinessWeek.* http://www.businessweek.com/articles/2013-05-09/the-right-way-for-a-ceo-to-deliver-bad-news

Trump Productions LLC, & Mark Burnett Productions. (2004). (Producer). *The Apprentice.* Atlantic City: NBC.

About the Author

For Dr. Santo D. Marabella, teaching has always been at the heart of his passion. And, practicing what he teaches – as a consultant, community organizer and now, a writer - is what gives voice to The Practical Prof. A real-life college management professor at Moravian College, Marabella enjoys being your personal work-life advisor.

A Professor of Management at Moravian College, Bethlehem, PA, Marabella received his undergraduate degree from Villanova University, an MBA from Erivan K. Haub School of Business at St. Joseph's University and a Doctor of Social Work from the University of Pennsylvania's School of Social Policy and Practice. His "practical" experience and consulting includes work and research in business management, social work, the performing arts and not-for-profit boards. In addition to his teaching, he has held a variety of leadership positions, both at the College and in the community. He founded, headed and leads a number of not-for-profit organizations and programs including a film commission, arts council and a community leadership program. He has consulted for, or spoken to, more than 75 regional and national organizations and companies. Even his research is "practical" – and includes creating an orientation program for new members of not for profit boards of directors and a model for training customer service personnel.

Currently, Marabella serves as: Film Commissioner for ReadingFilm, a division of the Greater Reading Convention & Visitors Bureau; Chair,

Alumni Council of the School of Social Policy & Practice at the University of Pennsylvania; and, Chair, Board of Trustees, Greater Reading Alliance of Community Theatres.

Other writing by Marabella include his plays "My Inside Out," a one-act play about self-discovery, "Baile, Abuela!", a two-act musical production showcasing salsa dance, "Senior Exploits" a play aimed at preventing scams among senior citizens, and "Symphony of Dreams," an original musical combining his script with songs written by his musician-father.

A native of Reading, PA, but born in Italy, Marabella is the only child of Anna & Sam – spoiled but not a brat (his words, not theirs), and resides in Fleetwood, with his fur-child, Rafaelle (pictured below), a flat-coated retriever who has been mostly patient during the writing of this book.

The Practical Prof and Rafaelle

www.ingramcontent.com/pod-product-compliance
Lightning Source LLC
Chambersburg PA
CBHW061607220326
41598CB00024BC/3479